DISSOLVING PLEASING OTHERS

Dissolving Pleasing Others dissolves childhood
blocks freeing you.

Robert A. Wilson

From me to the reader:

May your life forever flow—of lavish avalanches of bountiful
bliss in the right, loving way under grace of embraced love
and appreciation. Now and forever more may you soar, full of
wealthy health and sumptuous splendor.

May your life be as blessed as you are a blessing to me and the
world in a bright, bold, beautiful way.

I Love You and Thank You:
Robert A. Wilson
http://mycowboywisdom.com

ISBN 978-1-54399-002-7

© July 2016 by Robert A. Wilson/Cowboy Wisdom/Cowboy
Wisdom Publishing and Trademarked #Trademark Serial
number 86698406 by /Walk of Wisdom Webinars and Seminars
July, 2016

Cowboy Wisdom Publishing is a subsidiary of Cowboy Wisdom
Enterprises, LLC, publishes Cowboy Wisdom downloads, CD's,
Walk of Wisdom Webinars and Seminars Wisdom.

Thank you for purchasing **Dissolving Pleasing Others**.

Dissolving Pleasing Others focuses on the ways I expanded my life, to show you the way to expand yours. *Dissolving Pleasing Others* is written as a guide for you to discover who *you* are, *your* way. As I came to realize everything in life is temporary, I embedded everything within me, so I understand now is my time to dissolve—to release the knowledge and let go by appreciating that *I* am responsible for *everything* in my life; and by participating I am being accountable for all facets of my life. Through this, I appreciate that all my life experiences allow me to feel the emotional value of my life.

I wrote *Dissolving Pleasing Others* to allow people to utilize my life experiences as a guide to unlock and unblock himself or herself; to uncover and discover your talents, innovation, and paths of prosperity. Allowing my writings to show you a better way to experience life; allowing you the courage and savvy to unlock your childhood and allow your dreams to mature so they can be your new "way of life."

I dedicate this book to Mom, Dad, my siblings and all my family. As I now admit and tell the world I had the greatest parents with me, honouring them by admitting all my life is all *my* doing. As I now say to Mom, Dad, my siblings and all my family: Thank You. I love you for being my family as I now present to the world *Dissolving Pleasing Others* for *your* reading joy and pleasure.

CONTENTS

PREFACE

Dissolving Pleasing Others is written from my own personal awakening, realizing that I was living today through my childhood. I wrote this book in first person, yet these words come together as a guide to dissolve inner frustrations; to dissolve the need to please others that was embedded and ingrained through childhood experiences.

As I have come to understand over time, I grew up yet never matured. As I opened my valor to understand, I reacted and responded to life's situations just the way my parents allowed me to: realize it, admit it, and dissolve all. This book is written for people to let them know being perfect is not a goal. It is written to shine a light on understanding while growing up in a poverty-conscious household. As I now admit, my parents lived there the way they understood it. I now grasp, I embedded everything in my life and held on to all of it, thinking and believing that I was somehow betraying myself when I expanded out of something into something new.

This book is about understanding and dissolving the thought of living in ancestral habits, and adhering to the haunts, customs, and behaviors found there. As I grew up with an addiction in the household, I also realize and admit that I embedded and ingrained stuff that never ever had any affect on me in any way. As I grew up there was very little room for error and the grown-ups were always right. This book is about liberating the childhood and embellishing your enterprising abilities to experience your dreams. This book will allow you to expand out of that ingrained cocoon of childhood sights, scenes and sounds in order to mature into your real dreams and desires.

DISSOLVING PLEASING OTHERS

I asked myself: How did this statement instill my "pleasing others" mindset? *Color inside the lines to make Mom and Dad happy?*

I now understand...

Trying to please Mom, Dad, and school teachers instilled my pleasing others mentality that *I can now admit...*I dissolved it all.

I asked myself: *How does a statement make Mom and Dad proud?* Realizing that this was the cause of the beginning of embedding my pleasing others habits and behaviors.

I now ask myself: *How does dissolving pleasing others allow my inspirational innocence to excite my internal optimism?*

I also ask: *How does trying to please other people in a relationship begin to end the relationship or begin an ungrateful relationship and eventual heartbreak?*

When I awoke with this question: *How was I afraid to admit I tried to please others?*

As I delved deeper within me for the awakening, something appeared;

Something that cleared, cleansed, and polished my inner core to shine and gleam mirroring diamonds in the sunlight. I learned from my childhood to please others in an innocent way; so as a child, the outside, the chiding from others caused me to hide memories of the ridicule. Those memories were covered up and embedded deep within;

To travel with me through life experiences, creating the ways I responded or reacted emotionally in the moment;

And the way I feel and interpret the situation emotionally energizes my memories, beliefs, viewpoints, opinions, habits, and behaviors—imprinted patterns of responses and reactions from that atmosphere of every situation;

I stored everything in my memories that stimulates my emotions, feelings, thoughts, and responses;

Without me having a clue where everything begins, yet I see the outcomes by understanding that...

This I release trying to please others

To forthrightly and honestly speak my farsighted feelings and enterprising emotions to expand the wisdom for all participating.

So now I ask: *How do businesses fail by trying to please their big accounts and disregard small accounts?*

I also unleashed this question: *How is playing favoritism or trying to be the boss's favorite another way of trying to please others?*

And I ask: *How do I feel about dissolving pleasing people within me?*

I responded freely...liberated and emancipated as I asked myself: *How is pure, enterprising wisdom entering my dreamer's Zen?*

To never ever think, feel or respond by trying to please anybody and everybody allows me to begin investing in me, myself and I;

Listening to all ingenious lore and success savvy of others to energize my wise, expand my grandeur, and engage with my inner sage;

It electrifies my pioneering spirit to execute these experiences that allow and authorize me to feel, heed, and experience my life's glorious gusto;

The gusto that boldly and brightly bubbles up within me to polish my paths of peace, poise, prowess, and prosperity because I showed me, myself and I.

I encompassed the gutsy valor to cut my ties and stop trying to please others, admitting a job is nothing more than pleasing others with hidden signs.

Pity me distrusting my fellow workers because workers have a fear of trusting their own abilities and continuously are scared that they lack the ability to keep a job;

I now admit, relish, and fully understand that I never worried about a job or keeping my job.

I asked myself: *How is being job scared trying to please others steal my self-esteem show me myself and I my emotional insecurity?*

As I now admit, realize, and admire I encompass the ability to accomplish all the outcomes I wish with professional prowess;

This allows me to admit the solid fact that selfish arrogant workers tried to please the boss to their face, then, behind their backs, were the biggest screw-offs;

Ready to blame somebody else—one of their fellow workers— and the boss fell for it every time.

As I now heard my divine spine communication admitting and realizing I would work harder on my job for me, myself and I;

This allowed me to admit I would talk about my business at work and my job at home with others;

I never dissolved the worker within me to expand my freedom to facilitate feeling my power, to participate as *I* pleased.

People must feel wanted, they must feel the power of friendship and loyal valor instead of solely thinking "I need my weekly paycheck." For that binded my mind in work; the idea for the man to solely survive.

As I now realize and admit, working for the "man" paid the bills and everything, but: *How did working keep me in the "please pity me" game of life?*

I now realize a job is trying to please others because today, to keep a job, the bosses feel the employee has to kiss their backside in order to stay employed;

Because when a worker stands up they are called a trouble-maker. This shows me the lack of confidence in bosses and business owners today;

As I open my gut gallantry to grasp I was awakened with a kick-in-the-butt, showing me how I worked harder for others,

Than I worked for myself. This opened me to admitting the fact that working harder for others is trying to please others…always.

I now ask: *How is a job trying to please others and **all** fellow workers the same as trying to stay in harmony with them; trying to never create waves when something goes awry?*

Yet…I blemished and diminished my self-esteem because I kept everything bottled up until I got so fed up, I blew up at them.

I asked: *How did my selfish pride cover up trying to please others?*

As I now admit, understand, and embellish the joy and peace I feel by grasping, admitting and experiencing the wise willpower I have found.

I enjoy traveling the world, expanding peoples' lives with my inspirational wit;

Grasping **Cowboy Wisdom Enterprises, LLC** is, was, and always will be my pathway to my "Promised Land of Lavish Luxury."

Why? Because I now admit that I encompass the guts to query me, myself and I, to unblock my locks of pleasing others; to unleash the kapish of me, myself and I to fly.

To understand my enterprising entrepreneur embellishes my wisdom, innocence and inspirations, allowing me to experience the plush, lush gusto...

Of excellent health, lavish wealth, unselfish love for myself and for all people, mammoth money streams overfilling my bank accounts; and,

Elegantly experiencing all my divine grandeur and divine inheritance now and forever.

I understand there is always, in *all* ways, endless and bountiful bliss for me and all people; As I now grasp the fact that life is about liberation, emancipation, and freedom to explore and experience life through entrepreneurial endeavors, inspiration and innovation;

By trusting my abilities to innovate my innate inventive prowess; to make my life be *my* way of life.

I escaped from the hokey dupery of trying to please others as I asked this question: *How is trying to please others the same as trying to fit into a place I never belonged?*

As I watch and listen to my core cleverness and freedoms, I discovered that I tried to please others and ended up in a place I never fit in, because I was doing things to make myself fit that irked me internally.

Then...my internal fortitude excited my forthright valor to rise within me, myself and I;

> *Then I spoke aloud exactly how I felt.*
> *Then I offended somebody.*

I thought..."Oh, what did I do to deserve this dissident thinking?" instead of "Oh, well, what the hell1"

Because I now realize I kept things inside until I blew a gasket of brash candor to tell it just like it was;

Yet, deep inside I thought I hurt that person's feelings so I would then go and apologize for being who I am.

This was a sham of shame I placed upon myself as I realized I grew in age, yet I lacked maturity to expand my innovative grandeur;

All because I was too worried about what people would think of me if I failed.

As I realize trying to grasp what other people think is my fink of rinky-dink delusional despair within me, myself and I;

I now grasp the fact that I know what to do and that is the first step of staying the same—of staying who I am, being true to myself.

What other people think is step two in staying stuck in my poo—the stew of 'what do I do?'

Now step three is being afraid of uncertainty; scared to ride the trails of the terra incognita innocence within me because all dreams and desires and accomplished outcomes are inspirational innocence;

Showing me my internal, natural, nurturing optimism; canonizing enterprising nirvana candidly;

Expanding through the situation, staying unattached to everything I know or think to be true, thoughts of what other people think, with memories of what I think went wrong;

These are actually unlearned entrepreneurial insights; I saw all experiences with dark, discouraging blunder instead of thunderous temerity.

Temerity with lightning bolt power fissuring my stranglehold on my comfort zone of being a clone of my childhood school system;

What other people said, and feeling alone as I rode my trails of triumph.

I asked myself: *How is pleasing others smothering my dreams and desires?*

How is trying to please a partner in a relationship the end of a relationship?

I now admit, I tried to please the women when I was trying to get to know them;

This always ended badly and I walked away sad.

Looking at what was wrong with them embedded a blemish within me, myself, and I, until I admitted it was me trying to please them that brought about the blemish.

With this winner's wisdom gained, I unblemished me with this new awakening. I now concede that I took the job home with me, then got all wrapped up and over-wrought about what was happening on the job;

My thinking I was a big shot.

I now realize pleasing others runs deep within me from my childhood; my parents, too, brought the job home with them;

Then, at family functions, the job and what was wrong with said jobs was all that was talked about.

I now admit and understand that I do things the way my parents and people I thought were role models would do things;

This became embedded within me and I had to work for somebody harder than I had to work for myself.

I now expand my enterprising prowess.

I caught myself screwing around, playing on social media or checking out something on the phone, trying to become popular through my posts;

These were examples of me pilfering, wanting to be liked and pleasing others rather than getting done what I desired to do, a fault that has been my undoing pooh in the stew.

All my life, yes, I address this deeply and confess to the world; bless me for showing and expressing that I encompass the gall to look in my mirror of imprisonment and being smothered in pleasing others, because I now realize and admit pleasing others is always about, wondering and thinking: *What do people think of me?*

This is the stink of my falter fink within my skin.

I now realize it is easier to please others, yes, but thinking that by doing this I will make them like me is a lie, one that never dies.

All people do is take advantage of me. I admit that has happened; I have postponed what is right and bright for me, keeping me weeping and wimpy.

This has gone away now as I avow my **now** wowing feelings;

Heeding and experiencing my accomplished outcomes as I feel my breezes of bountiful bliss basking on my seashores of success.

Watching, sensing, and admiring my day-to-day splendor, I fill my life now and forever of Divine Order in bright, enlightened ways!

DISSOLVING MY ENSLAVING CODES

I ask myself: *How does the world today **still** have enslaving encryptions and oppressing codes that cause ones to believe: I must control people?*

As I look at the leaders of the world today, and the fascist way of life, now I ask: *How has everything in the world advanced except the way people communicate, listen and interact with each other?*

I asked myself: *How is trying to look like a big shot in other's eyes actually just me despising the cleverness and wisdom of...me?*

This sent me on a freedom march within my own skin to realize that within me is DNA of enslaving codes; codes teaching me that I must conquer some*thing* or some*body* are being lost tossed and bossed by my self-encrypted, enslaved mindset;

This mindset is one that encompasses all people of the world today because the world still believes in suppressing the working class in unsavory conditions;

Enslaving, conquering—a controlling travesty of justice that blemishes the minds of people;

Making them believe that they are superior to others is smothered in my funky feelings, punkie emotions, and self-centered inferiority to others; using scared arrogance to cover up their inner ignorance.

Using "bossing domination" over others is poverty paucity that keeps the world stuck in ancestral anger, pandering to famine, pillage, plunder and war;

Four vices that have raged on since the beginning of time are now forever gone within *me* because the world and all its people are opening their enterprising wise, filling the world with gifts of enterprising endeavors forever more.

The world soars, peace and prosperity thrill the world airwaves with boldofme bravery, freeing all in the Universe.

I asked myself: *How is life a conquering control of enslaved codes embedding the thought that 'I must control the world and all its wealth through pillage, plunder, famine and war' a lesson that history teaches?*

As I open my *numen* (my "guiding force") nirvana, I admit to the world I thought I had to be smarter; I had to think I knew more, wanted people to like me, and wanted everything done my way;

These were my chains; these encryptions of my controlling arrogance that created the anger, frustration and insecurities in me, myself and I.

This was an internal lie I told myself; I kept repeating the sham and damned what was wrong with them and blemished my life in every way.

As I awakened, I harkened my internal innocence instantly and opened my sunrise-eyes to see a new dawn of daring, audacious wisdom;

I nurtured my listening-'preneur' leadership; hearing my day to day escapades awakened my ascending, wise acumen;

Kinetically energized my natural gallantry to grasp that:

I am the best because I dissolved my enslaving codes, opening my revolutionizing resolve!

Understanding, conceding, and dissolving the deeply hidden enslaving codes of my ancestral tyranny, that I must control others with conquering controlling;

This means I now grasp the truth. I think, thought and memorized enslaving barriers, the ones that taught me I must harass and ridicule others.

Thinking I was smart was a lie I told myself. To honor me, I now admit and concede I was a peevish pauper spewing my dipshit thinking.

I now realize and admit the world still churns and burns in enslaved codes that goad people into thinking they are more important than they are.

I now realize and admit, to me and the rest of the world, my own inherited illiteracy of enslaved enigmas that held emotional control over me...have gone away;

Because I now see, feel, and enjoy my new ways of understanding life through listening-'preneurial' innocence;

Feeling emancipated from my enslaved codes that galled me into anger, frustration and bitterness toward others; I feel free from my blither-blathering, smothered in oppressed anger from ingrained patterns of pompous paucity codes.

I now understand and declare: I rooted in dimwitted enslaved conceit and was released. I admirably unlocked this block within me today and have now opened my nirvana understanding.

Since the beginning of time, I encompassed subconscious limitations that included enslaved conceit and enslaved encryptions embedded in my DNA and past lives;

Although...I now open my eternal eyes and my listened-'preneur' to dissolve my enslaved conceit that stemmed from the belief that I must conquer others.

11

That same belief that was inanely encrypted in all people since the beginning of time. Believing in the enigmas of pillage, plunder, and war continue to control peoples' food supply;

Believing these are the devices to rule the world is ancestral anarchy. It makes people today believe that they must be the boss of others to feel emotionally adequate in their own existence.

I felt that once. But I now understand that I stayed stuck in my enslaved arrogance because my thoughts surrounded a core of self-conceit…thinking I was helping.

Thinking I could help people was a sham; it was a conquering mind that blinded me into thinking I was the leader. This was mis-leading thinking within me, because I now understand that, to be the leader I must listen to people with my listened-'preneur' in order to hear their individualism.

To grasp this, I now understand it is arrogance that tells people what to do and how to live their lives. An arrogance that left me, myself and I, the instant I admitted and realized;

Arrogance is stuck in the crevices of what I know locks and blocks me, myself and I, in my memories of self-deception that I ingrained within me because I thought for a time that life was against me.

This was a chilling calamity until I taught myself; until I sharply opened me, myself and I, up to realizing and admitting that my sover-eign savvy shows people the way to expand through life, feeling their thriving traveler's temerity;

As I express the wisdom I attained from my own life experiences so they can better understand and admit for themselves that they will never ever know the way to my results without seeing those results;

This truth unlocks my lionized lore and shows me my self-as-sured autonomous acumen:

I Zenned from listening to my daily escapades; to be a lis-
tened-'preneur' and feel my self-assured gallantry.

To concede that I dissolved my past because I stopped trying to heal a memory, opens me up to recognize the fact that my daily jaunts unlock my blocks;

The blocks placed in my memories. I now grasp today's events are showing me the way to release my ingrained memories by ordaining the wisdom of that event within my daily activities;

I have now awoken and understand life expands as I hear, heed and admire my emotional fruition of inspired insight gained from every event that ever occurred within my life, actuating my innate potentate prowess.

Now and forever, I bask in the bliss of my bright, luminescent, inspirational splendor—sensationalizing my feelings of copious cornucopia glowing from core décor as I illuminate my Milky Way—tasting life as the rich, milk chocolate of my dreamer's upshots; tantalizing fabulous pleasure to be my way of life…

Today and every day;
Under the grace of esteemed elegance forever;
And of Divine Order in a free, flowing way.

FISSURING
ANCESTRAL ATTACHMENT

I asked myself: *How liberated and innocent will I feel by detaching from all habits, behaviors and customs of my ancestors?*

I now realize, admit and heed the fact, I encompass ancestral behaviors, habits and ways of life by...admitting this.

I begin to dissolve this through my inner awakenings; to see how my ancestors, parents, school, and I, instilled my ancestors' way of life, as I now liberate myself.

To liberate all today, I still encompass my ancestors' survival mindset as I heed the world events and my way of life that was instilled when I was a child.

So, I ask: *How does the world think it has advanced, yet stay stuck in ancestral survival mode?*

As people ridicule anybody and everybody that shows the desire to expand out of "ancestral patterns," to survive incapacitation through innovative ideas liberating themselves from ancestral ways of life.

I asked once: *Is ancestral survival mode the underlying reason for people to dislike people of wealth and think they control other peoples' lives?*

I asked: *Is the reason people of wealth think they own workers because ancestral anarchy has taught the wealthy that they are higher than the working and the middle class?*

Today, I ask: *Does the world **still** subconsciously utilize an enslaving mindset that mirrors our ancestors and oppressors throughout history?*

As I now unlock this block, I realize people think of others like cattle today because when somebody works, somebody bosses. Said bosses subconsciously think to themselves, "I own them," which is corporate cloning that descended from a school system of historical bondage.

The belief that "I must conquer and own," is cloned in all people through our DNA subconscious mind and history.

I now cleared, cleansed and cleaned my ancestral cloned anarchy from within me, and now feel my life's liberated innocence freeing every cell inside me, allowing me to see that:

I am the innovator of innocent inspirations!

I am the one to expand people and show them their path through life by unlocking their trendsetting talent. Now and forever more, I soar of sovereign omnipotent audacity, realizing and proclaiming people possess the divine right to express and activate their;

Wisdom, innovation, and talent with a electro magnetic motion magnetizing the universe airwaves 24/7 displaying their moneyed up consummated upshots in the right, superb way;

With blessings from me to all and from all to me, myself and I, under grace of love, appreciation, facilitation, participation, and a gracious thank you;

As I am one with my dreams, now and forever, I thank you. I love you. I am sorry. Please forgive me, thank you as I grasp and admit that

NOW is the time for me to dissolve, release and let go of all attachments to my ancestors' way of life.

As I now heed and experience life, I see yesterday the same as today, because the powers to be feel they have to control people through poverty and selfish power;

This shows me the leaders of today are powerless and clueless internally, because controlling people through laws and taxation;

Thinking entitlements help people, is a disenabling fallacy.

I now feel and admit I dissolved my ancestral haunts within in me myself and I with ease and grace of embraced love and appreciation, liberates me, myself and I to thrive in autonomous triumph;

I now admit and heed that entitlements are given, so the politicians feel they are entitled to everything the populace works for. This promptly inspires desires to be awoken today;

And I ask this question: *How are my beliefs, viewpoints, opinions, and history a mirage that forms an attachment between people behaviors, habits, traditions today and our ancestors' behaviors, habits, and traditions?*

As I asked myself today: *How is the world **still** attached to our ancestor's survival modus operandi, yet timidly thinking we are doing better?*

As I asked myself today: *How does present day mirror the beginning of time through out the world?*

As I open my internal innovative wit, I see the world has advanced in medicine and technology;

Yet the way people are treated throughout the world, and in the workplace, is the exact same as it was in the beginning of time;

As I heed the rhetoric, people with money want to exercise their power and keep taking the quality of life from others;

People with money and power are in power positions, and only seem to want more money and power;

Therefore, power mongers surrender the real business morals and ethics for the fake-and-bake power of money.

I now realize people with inner strength always feel confident, just as power mongers feel insecure and disrespect themselves internally, stinking of thinking that money gives them power and respect;

But...it's the position that gives them power. All power positions encompass a moral and ethical value; a demand for respect;

Yet these people who hold them always end up on the short end of the stick, licking their wounds of immorality, begging for forgiveness from others;

Yet, forever they live with internal 'ick.'

Still today, because they have the same "everything is mine" mindset as our ancestors once held dear.

So, I ask myself: *How are the leaders of today stuck on the money and power rather than the morals and ethics of their positions for the good of all people?*

A country that is morally and ethically bankrupt soon becomes a boondoggle of financial bankruptcy.

How do you see that fact occurring in the world today, and also since the beginning of time, I ask all people?

Like me, I heed worldly events. The leaders of the world and people still think war settles conflicts, yet I now understand history and 'war colleges' create incapable leaders;

Because leaders want respect fro the people by wanting those same people to see them as wise and secure within themselves, yet through their leadership actions and ideas show their tyrannical incompetency ending in revolting way.

Grasp, as I do now, that physical power is powerless paucity within their core turncoat; insecure leaders are too scared to trust their own abilities; self-doubting leaders are too terrified to bring about accomplished outcomes to expand peoples' lives;

Because leaders who operate with feeble belief systems of self-centered conceit, stomp on people with the power of their position and outside sources; such as, political office military and police forces.

As I ask... *How do I observe these traits in the leaders of the world today?*

As I now look at today and back through history, I ask myself: *How are the same places in the world mired in the same turmoil now as they were yesterday or yesteryear?*

To open my optimistic omnipotence, to feel my unconquerable wisdom of innocence, to feel the world's prospering prowess of the people;

I now understand, since the beginning of time until today, leaders of the world were and remain afraid of the wisdom and courage of the people.

That is the reason for laws of listlessness, because I now understand my ancestors lived in the fear of those in power until those in power forget the power of people banning together to achieve a common accomplished outcome.

I now grasp it is the arrogance of leaders that cause their downfall. Through thinking and believing they control peoples' lives, other countries, and worldly affairs, has been the downfall of *all* listless leaders since the beginning of time.

So, I ask: *How are the same arrogant leadership styles still occurring today throughout the world?*

As I now concede and release, I grasp and admire the fact that the entrepreneurs of the world will lead the world to peace and prosperity; excusing the wannabe leaders from the worldly landscape in the right, loving way, under grace of enterprising exuberance;

Because I now understand a trendsetting leader listens, expands affluence within the populace with a trailblazer's enlightened wit;

As I open my eyes to see and hear I am a leader of listening lithe to hear all that is occurring around me sets me free to feel my "inspirational lore" *light up my heart temerity and soul splendor for evermore.*

As a wise affluent leader allows people to live a life they desire to experience because an *entrepreneurial populace* is at peace within looking for "enterprising adventures."

As I now understand, I realize my ancestors understood hard work and minimal pay was the way; As I ask… How is hard work and minimal pay still in the world and bosses minds today?

I now realize my ancestors blazed trails of triumph for the world to experience an explorer epiphany within, because today, with modern technology, they can span the globe within seconds with a worldly base of bliss and ascend to success every day.

I ask myself: *How do my ancestors still control my life?*

As I now open my gut willpower to look deep into the core of me, through my recollections;

Dismissing them from my life, I liberate myself from all my inherited and ancestral haunts that subconsciously directed my life;

Allowing myself to feel and be liberated and alive; to thrive in enlivened, enterprising energies; to feel my present moment prowess;

To saunter in endless, lavish abundances that dance with me as I scamper of a heavenly of sumptuous bliss;

As I sit in my rocking chair jovially enjoying life's simple, posh pleasures; understanding every breath is my timeless treasure of love, appreciation, facilitation, and participation of all phases of my amazing life...

*Feeling and embellishing my open heart and unleashed soul,
to enjoy my life today and every day, in every way, under grace,
in an excellent, elegant way and of Divine order now.*

Thank you. I love you all.

MY MANIPULATION OF ME
Cowboy Wisdom/Robert A. Wilson

I now resolutely recognize *everything* I do inside me that is unsavory is my pilfering manipulation from my immature arrogance and trained patterns controlling me.

As I mature, I facilitate everything inside me with an expression of expansionism. To understand 'ism' unleashes inspirational, spiritual, maharishi wit;

This unsheathes my wisdom, releasing innovative talent, and allows me to expand out of manipulation;

My understanding that "manipulation" began by my parents, when they said: "Rob, you do this, and we will give this."

This author-wized me to ask: *How did that begin their manipulation of me and me carrying that manipulation onto others?*

This opened me to understand life is manipulating—a professor teaching, "What's on the surface suffices for conscious vices;"

Yet the underneath sneaks in a meek miser to stay within my comfort zone fences keeping me dilated in despair.

I now understand minds are binded in despair, as the gut is the home of my 'dreamers dare,' unleashes my frontiersman flair;

Frees my inspiration; facilitates thinking; manipulates controlling vices of advice from all beliefs, viewpoints and encrypted etches of yesterday;

Cementing me into my retentions of preventions that I candidly concede I did only out of needy seediness, to fit into the daily routine of my wanting a safe and secure life;

Instantly awoken, hell-bent for election champion campaigner that understood life is to be performed at Olympian Fame;

Ordains my invincible innovator to blow reveille, feeling my facilitator go-getter, unfettered enterpriser lore, to understand people have been taught to manipulate;

To get ahead in their thought process which keeps the poverty-stricken fool bound up in all of us, because we look around at the material chattels.

Everybody else rattled my cage of rage that cast me procrastination and shimmied away the instant my Zorro Zeal arrived on the scene;

Slicing a 'Z' right across the situation zeroed out the doubt; Zenned my zillionaire zest by televising my sassy fervor.

So, I asked myself: *How are my embedded boundaries manipulating me to think what other person should do and this is the way they ought live their life were my controlling 'thoughts?'*

This question got instantly wrung-out, ringing in the whims of "I won;"

Appreciating the person for their participation to expand my resolve;

To evolve through situations unbridled my stouthearted admittance to ask: *How do boundaries and forgiveness embed my 'victim-I-tice?'*

A question that enticed me to divulge the expanded expression of appreciation of everything; to heed, feel, and experience the vibrant value of every circumdance enhances my daring dance of visionary veracity.

How do boundaries allow me to escape responsibility and accountability to respect the other person's desires, and the way they desire to live their life?

How does thinking *having thoughts or unsavory memories about anybody or anything in my internal landscape, create inner angst that has me focusing on them rather than on my dreams?*

These questions instantly unlocked me, myself and I, as I authorized all of 'them' to be promptly dissolved, released, and let go;

Ditching the boundaries that come with unsettling people or events flat out explains to me that I allowed outside sources to chide and manipulate me;

By this confession, I addressed my ascending acumen, blessing me, myself and I, and giving 'them' permission to feel my emotional emancipation; sensualizing my inspirational spirited moxie;

As I now boldly divulge to me, myself and I that my live-out-loud power is a good thing, as I now expand through life by loving appreciating, facilitating, and participating in every event, with feeling heeding and experiencing life-expanding value from every situation, because heartbreaks, jealousy, and other negative expectations are my controlling manipulators;

Embedded from my manipulating mindset that blinded me into thinking people and life should absolutely go my way *every* time I whined in all my discouraging dismay;

The whine I admit I once displayed within my inner landscape has now blown away, into oblivion, as my luminary life arrives, enlivens and thrives;

Filled with newborn nuances; a nurturing numen nirvana within my innovator's skin of the "I won" valor.

I now admit and understand, my life experience's fissure and dissolve my memory; of my mind manipulation of me, myself and I, as I purely cleaned my memories;

Crisply cleansed my thoughts purely cleared my visions, and pristinely shined my Divine prescience [*presh-uh ns-ee-uh-ns*] intuits my Divine spine sensations;

Tantalized pacesetter prowess allows me to avow my vows of visionary omnificent wisdom, sensualizing my celestial wise to rise from within;

Me, Myself and I, now and forever more.

My optimistic resolve energizes my emotional enterprising endeavors.

As I now dissolve the impish involvement of my memory mind that manipulated me, making me see myself as a pawn of bondage when, in fact, I am a free man;

As I am liberated—ecstatically emancipated supreme today and forever more, because I heeded and adhered to my daredevil desire;

A desire that inspires my fiery sprees of splendor, ascending my gut sovereignty to never defend a point of view to disturb the hue that my new painting of poetic peace and plush prosperity excites.

My dauntless desire to be trusting facilitator, listening to glisten new wisdom. As I hearken my fresh, keen wit, the cosmic clairvoyants are expressing to me to free myself eternally, externally, and internally, in wise, wonderful ways;

As I ruthlessly admit to the universe and *all* people: I manipulated me, myself and I, and I now admit I am the only one who can manipulate me; the only one who has the power to do so.

I admit it and dissolve it all through my gallant gall to experience it all.

Because the simplicity of life, looking internally and freeing eternity, has me now confessing my penitence of paucity that gnawed at me internally.

I unleash my kevalin kapish because I honor myself to appreciate all my life expanding events of today.

Because today I was poked, and awoke to ask myself: *How is my thinking memory mind the manipulator of me?*

Then, I asked: *How does my thinking memory mind deceive me, keeping me in the doldrums of ho-hum and keeping me stuck in the ancestral muck?*

With this, I unlocked a block: All that has happened in my life—good, bad or indifferent—is the way my life occurred.

Yet I now have the guts to admit the way I expanded through it all was by appreciating everything and everybody;

I stopped accepting shrinking down to the level of others, dissolving my bondage that had me stuck in forgiveness-setting boundaries, and accept that I herded for others who are smothered in herd-o-cracy;

I concede that I bowed down to that stuff I now declare was me coddling myself to look for sympathy, and I admit today I was good at it, as I now mature to understand manipulation, anger, frustration, and jealousy was a package of 'victim-I-tice.'

It was 'crap-I-tice' that was my thinking mind manipulating impish, nagging delusions;

Polluting me because I knuckled under to the pity-me palaver and my imp of dim, because I looked at my life through pitying, self-retaliation;

Thinking the world was against my pity-me-I-tice, looking at the world through eyes of despising envy. Thinking everybody has everything but me;

This thinking was *me, myself and I* deceiving *me, myself and I* again, as I now understand my life experiences are my legacy ecstasies;

This inspired 'visionary' eternal dreams, as I now grasp all my thoughts of despair was simply my thinking mind binding me to memory, slurring my life with deceiving peevishness stuffed with my selfish arrogance;

My creepy cheater was beating me up internally and I expressed my pity-a-tion of self-relation to the world, to free all people as now I stand before the world and confess:

My pity-a-tion of my self-retaliation of me addressing all the people with sovereign savvy; this comes from people thinking memory mind is the manipulator of their lives, good, bad or whatever.

I now concede after pulling the weeds, how I manipulated myself with my memories, wants and needs.

Now, as I look at my life, I understand the physical world is a manipulation of education, encodings, ancestral encryptions, self-taught negatives, and trying to fit in and please people;

I realized the manipulation of my thinking thoughts and mind to unwind my exquisite ecstasies;

To feel the universe's ultra-utopia frequencies of "easy street feats."

Feeling my esteemed energy flowing and glowing from within me;

Heating the world with my heart and soul; summer-y spectaculars that light up my life like the fireworks on the 4th of July;

As my sunrise surprises rise over the horizon, I feel my sumptuous splendor arrive and thrive in my daily life; in bright, golden, glowing, gleeful ways.

As I now realize my goldmine is within me, it un-seizes my easy, free streaming, cascading cash flow that glows so bright from bank accounts, now and forever, in the right blessed way.

In a love under grace, in plush prosperous ways,
and in Divine order
now and forever.
I glow of glorious gusto!

I STOPPED THINKING I LOOK GOOD IN OTHER'S EYES

I asked me: *How liberated do I feel the instant I stopped thinking I look good in other's eyes exulting heeding and feeling my new emancipated emotions?*

Grasping this fresh wizardry, I freed myself from looking good in other's eyes.

I stopped "thinking" I looked good in other people's eyes to feel I am outré omnipotent, dissolving all boundaries within me.

I blatantly asked myself: *How do I talk big; wanting people to think I'm a 'big thinker' makes me believe I look good in other peoples eyes?*

By asking this, I opened me, myself and I, to stare straight into my mirror of honor and integrity;

This allowed me to stop thinking big because I now admit, fathom, and declare that thinking big is a letdown, because thinking is a mind thing minus the core chutzpah;

I say I got it; the intestinal fortitude to now realize, heed and declare that without the internal oomph everything goes up in a smoke of a hoax;

Because I now understand and declare my rococo inspirations excite my hell-raiser reveries and unleash my clever candor to expand through life;

Energizes my gut gallantry, innerprizes my visionary veracity enterprise, my wizardry wise to execute my entrepreneurial experiences;

To heed, experience and free my accomplished outcomes internally, bubbling full with my glorious galvanized gusto, now and forever more.

I now show, feel, and experience the vim and vigor of me, myself and I, as I encompass the gut gallantry to look me, myself and I in the eye;

To fly, because to think big and look good is something I'm doing for outside sources has opened me up to feel my empowering forces;

As I promptly showed me, myself, and I, allowing *all* people to heed my experiences;

Watch and witness me "walk my talk," showing them my spry, ingenious valor.

As I now correspond with other people, I sharply listen with a lithe ear to hear the wisdom and innovative inspirations from others to expand me, myself and I;

By enhancing my ingenious inspirations; to enjoy my ride of riches, today and every day, in bold, beautiful way!

As I opened my inner Pandora's box, unhooking the bragger's hoax within me, myself and I, I presented my gallant gall to ask: *How do I do things to look good in other people's eyes?*

Then I was looking deeper into myself...

To uncover and discover my self-centered, controlling troll that kept me wondering what other people think of me and how would they do the task I just did was the pooh, in my doo-petty-doo, stew thinking stuck in the quandary of my internal dirty laundry.

As I heard, I'm big thinker; I think big, yet there was a deep rumbling, bumbling, mumble of pansy palaver deep within my gut allowing me to admit that I think big yet I felt small;

Small and insecure internally. I now understand and declare that I can think big and talk big with my excuses wiggling my waggling my tail of failure; yet, internally, I was telling me, myself and I otherwise;

I ruthlessly concede I was full of doubletalk; balking and talking; feeling couch potato-I-tice, which all went away the instant I felt the courage to feel the power of my heart voltage and soul amperage;

Energizing my visionary frequencies to see, feel, and grasp my emotional empowering energies are my powerhouse of prowess;

Omnificence wisdom, enterprising revelations heralding omnipotent utopian savvy, every day.

I now realize, admit and dissolve my clichés that being a big thinker is nothing but me wanting and needing people to hear and see it.

I now broadened my rainbow resolve to show my charismatic colors;

Blasting across the heavenly skies, beaming my adventurous entrancing portraits of my dreams, desires and accomplished outcomes;

Aggrandizing and galvanizing my dynamic desires to experience my affluent, amazing, accomplished outcomes because I encompass the guts to admit "thinking big is a façade;"

Dodging, dealing with my moping mocking memories that bind my feelings, emotions and subconscious mind into whatever I embedded through my beliefs, thoughts, interpretations, perceptions, moods, and everything involved to understand that thinking big sounds good…

To my self-centered, know-it-all, yet I felt timid;

I feel tiny deep within me, myself and I because I now understand my outcomes are directly proportioned to my emotional energy, gut feelings, and the effort I put forth to accomplish my desired outcome.

I now grasp to think big and talk big was my own needy greedy arrogance, wanting people to think good things about me means doing everything for somebody else.

I now heed to be of my received riches; I show myself that I have gut sovereign splendor and audacity to walk my paths of progressive prosperity, willing to fissure limiting beliefs, opinions and viewpoints;

Thinking thoughts of my memory mind.

So, I asked myself: *How is thinking big a "feel good, look good" in other people's eyes allowing others to take advantage of me and have them thinking I come to them at their beck-and-call?*

As I now admit and dissolve, I have been there, done that, face down splat, feeling like crap, went to oblivion.

I now realize, I think and talk myself out of everything only to then justify within my limiting beliefs, thoughts, opinions and viewpoints.

Then I puff up my chest, thinking I look good with a bragger's shortcomings, talking a big story to the world;

Thinking I look good in other people's eyes created an inner crying; feeling shy and denying everything because my talk never matched my outcomes;

Within my internal honor I understood I could do it, yet I lacked the gallant gall to admit where my thought processes began;

As I now have stopped resisting to admitting the fact...I was hiding.

From my childhood stuff, trying to bluff the world and all people, yet in my innermost ghost I hosted a chiding, clamoring dialog of my insecurities.

31

As I now declare and recognize I play the part of the smartass to cover up things in my life.

As I now feel at peace with me, myself and I, I now grasp and declare that thoughts and memories of looking good in other peoples' eyes is gone, like sundown;

I opened my profound cutting-edge leadership skills to expand of peace, patience, poise, prowess, and prosperity;

I exhilarated my individual expansionism of intrepid, sagacious moxie to participate and facilitate my life;

Divulging and grasping that to think is to hide in my knowing; to understand excites my innermost mastery.

So I stopped thinking big to expand feeling my visionary zeal, exciting my farseeing curiosity, sensing my worldly-wise dynamism, and exhilarating my life's innocent pleasures to understand and grasp I think in happiness;

As I sense, I feel of peace and understand peace parades eternal ardor communions every day;

As I now grasp to feel and experience the dynamics of my life, I unthink what I know in order to feel my core spirit;

Voices éclat (*success*) revelations, virtuously engendering trend-setting wisdom to flow from deep within, unhooking my thinking in happy thoughts;

To feeling my feisty, exultant, emotional lore; illuminating natural gifts to beam from innermost omnific animations that allow me to live and feel infinite bliss;

Allows me to feel my lust for life's luminous, inspirational fervency;

Allowed me to enjoy life from core peace, praising every day amazing stellar élans.

As I now understand, thinking big is to think in competition and I own good enough guff.

As I now avow, I understand valuing my winner's wit to succeed in whatever I desire to experience, because I now grasp I am endowed with inspirational wisdom, intuitive innovation, and trailblazing talent that allows me to feel appreciation—I feel gracious.

Expressing "thank you" for everything in my life shows me I embolden the glorious gut valor to understand and concede, I put things off until tomorrow, which stems from childhood.

I asked myself: *How did my getting by with doing things as a kid stop me from living my dreams now?*

As I admit, I would try to get out of everything; and I did get out of a lot of things because my parents would do it for me, or I would con another into doing it for me; yet this was a slight of hand con job I did to me, myself and I.

As I admit to get rid of it once and for all, sometimes I would do it thinking I was getting even with somebody else, or with my parents, which was my selfish brat crap;

When I thought these thoughts, I thought I was being clever, and was severing my "get-it-done!" attitude. I was being a brat that went splat, because I thought I was getting by with something.

I was getting by with being lazy and lying to myself, and now I grasp my childhood was more than just getting a high school diploma and going out on my own without realizing and admitting I was cloned by my childhood;

As I now admit to me, myself and I—all people and the universe—I embedded ways to look at the world through blaming eyes and shaming ears because I watched and learned how to finagle my way through life by putting off things;

Things that always, in all ways, come back to bite me in my wannabe tough guy butt.

So by being ruthlessly honest and forthright with me, myself and I, I author-'wize' me to grasp that I am now liberated to begin and embellish my inner expansionism of inspirations superstar mojo exciting my grit get and go;

I now realize my life was set in motion from childhood up to now, as I would try to slide by putting off school work;

Trying to get out of what my parents asked me to do was the beginning of my poo in the stew of never do.

Because I now see where these self-embedded dreads are the way I live today when it pertains to dreams, desires, and accomplished outcomes;

Because I learned to put things, as I now admit and realize, everything I thought was cunning as childhood is faulting halt of clamoring clutter today;

Because I now grasp that my childhood was set in stone as I got out on my own, without my parents and everything else;

Because I thought I knew everything and that caused me to put off things until later.

Now I admit they never ever got done. It was me shunning my abilities, dreams and integrity;

The lazier in the maze mediocrity I became embedding inane mundane my life became went away in a blaze of brazen boldofme freedom.

As I now waltz with my dreamer's desires and moneyed-up accomplished outcomes;

As I now feel my shining star of sumptuous success beam from within me, embellishing my third eye that watches me travel the world in spectacular style, sitting on my Riviera of copious riches;

As I now feel my excellent health, windfalls of lavish luxury fill my life today and every day in every way, under grace of love, appreciation, participation and...

Thank You!
Of divine order, now and forever.

INTRODUCTION
TO EXPANSIONISM

As you read…*feel* the words rather than *know* the words in order to expand your life, see your way free of knowing, to expand of understanding newfound freedom within.

I now introduce the simplicity of expansionism; introducing all people to expand, energize, enterprise, and experience because these words are *free* of memorized thinking, feelings, and emotions that enter into words having memory, such as, *change*;

Because *change* creates conscious and subconscious mind unrest, because of memorized undesirable experiences that enter the conscious mind from other events in life;

As *expand* is grand, because *expand* opens a pioneering passion within, as words such as; expand, energize, enterprise, and experience are liberated from memory: I am now the explorer of expansionism sensing *internal spectacular magnificence*. I see me free forever more;

As I now introduce all people to expansionism, inside me I see magnificent, invigorating, savvy, magical, imaginative subliminal miracles;

Innovate, sumptuous money streams flowing to me, myself and I, as I overfill my bank accounts with ease because I see money as energy from my accomplished outcomes;

This inspires spiritual miracles to occur within all phases of my amazing life, as I now understand, expansionism liberates my thinking in *change*; heal, create, transformation and expectations that are connected to memories;

As I now know everything that occurs in the physical world first occurs within me, myself, and I–I sense my emotional enterprising expressions speak uniquely to me;

Allowing me to quantify the wizardry within my life events and query the fury to uncover and discover my new frontiersman utopian revelations;

Which jazzes my newfound victorious valor and awakens my stalwart willpower to expand, energize, enterprise, and experience my daily escapades with my desired outcomes, as my engendering expansionism;

As whatever clever idea or issue is occurring in my life now, as I put forth facilitating foresight and effrontery enthusiasm to feel observe and experience my highest accomplished outcomes.

Because I now grasp *change* heals and creates, transformation and expectations are sideways thinking from memories;

Just rearranging tarnished furniture of what I already know to feel good about my life from a different view, yet encompassing the same sensitive dispiritedness;

Thinking good, yet feeling froze over internally—emotionally going through the motions of life.

As I now feel and adhere to my lionized, liberated expansionism, I sense magnanimous tenacity;

Because I now grasp, realize, and admit to expand leaves the old behind, freeing me from my subconscious mind to feeling my subconscious stimuli, which enhances my sagacious savvy to sense my heart and soul feel elegantly alive;

Like a beehive buzzing my bright, unadulterated, zillionaire zeal with sassy, sexy appeal exalts my spicy sagacity;

Sensing my innate spectacular, megastar mettle to stop meddling in yesterday's pity-me palaver instantly went away, authorizing me to unfreeze my easy street feats of financial ecstasy to understand expectations create anger;

As facilitating my day shows me focus, action, and candor it innovates lively, ingenious, torchbearer acumen;

Tantalizing internal newborn grandeur, surrendering my know-it-all crawling crap as I am free!

Because I unhooked my book learning to expand into and through life, as I now explain expansionism disconnects me from thinking mired in memories and what I already know;

Because the experience of expansionism occurred as I opened up to show people all my stuff I had wanted to hide from society, I liberated my life.

Then, as I began my journey, I got hooked into trying to change, heal, create transformation, forgiveness and expectations, until I realized that alley was a dead end and kept me stuck in the same place, always looking outside myself, overthinking everything while my life stayed the same internally in every way.

Ass I was always feeling stuck in my free-falling, recalling everything, trying to change, heal, create, and transform went away in an innocent way as I audaciously opened a new way of experiencing life;

A way free of memory because I now understand all the turmoil I *think* I sense in the physical world, lies within my thoughts, memories and thinking;

Especially as I would think, "what will other people say about me" went away as I began my understanding of expansionism.

Inside me is where I feel the emotional elegance of my lionized life dance as I liberated my internal feelings, expressing and relishing my gall to listen to my seers and sages of endearing insights of innocence, nurturing savvy, intuitive genius, harmonizing today's sensational events;

As I introduced myself to my visionary vocabulary of expand, energize, enterprise, and experience, it opened trails of triumph because I unhooked my past to avow my now to naturally optimize wisdom within me;

Forgetting to look at any outside source, to understand clearly that everything I desired to expand out of was inside me, and everything I desired to expand of was within my 'listenedpreneur.'

Prowess to hear all my sources of the universe speak uniquely to me, myself and I; to be free, emancipated, and liberated to enjoy my paths of expansionism;

Internalize simple trendsetting hegemony, seeing life, expanding wisdom throughout life, and simply expressing all my hidden stuff to the external world instantly dissolves, releases and let's go, liberating me from my old way of life.

Opening my listening lore allures my self-assured bravery to expand through the situation, trusting my amazing abilities to appreciate brilliant intuitive lore;

Lionizing, torchbearer, innovative, emotional savvy to understand I cleansed, cleaned, cleared, and polished my emotional energies of yesterday's tarnished tribulations;

Because I now admit, I taught myself selfish sabotage stuck in a system of snobbish greed with me needing to have more than everybody else was my paralyzing pity-me thinking; a thinking that went down the drain with all my self-taught agony;

Because the simple roads to resolve are to admit, realize, and take 100% responsibility that I allowed everything in my life;

I am 100% accountable for my actions and understand I permitted everything that happened in my life.

I did it to myself because of my bullheaded brat-I-ness; that everything about my life had to go my way or it was wrong was self-sabotaging silliness that I used and abused me with internally;

This went away instantly, as I now understand, heed, and feel my internal, eternal and physical expansionism of inspirational spiritual miracles that entice my mystical Mecca of magical intuition, and excite my innovative wit to waltz inspired temerity through all phases of my life;

To illuminate my geysers of glitz, to heed my blitzing brilliance of my celebrated pleasure as I effortlessly expand, energize, and enterprise my life experiences with glitzy grandeur from my heart and soul.

As I walk down Broadway basking in lavish, endless windfalls of Divine grandeur and of Divine Order evermore, my charisma beams my will of thrilling humility for all to enjoy!

ABOUT THE AUTHOR

I AM ROBERT A. WILSON with *Cowboy Wisdom Walk of Wisdom Webinars/Walk of Wisdom Seminars* Hypnotherapist, Dream Sculptor Cowboy Wisdom Publisher and published author.

I write and speak about the way I expanded my life, the ways I liberated my emotions and feelings from all my self-embedded stuff.

Cowboy Wisdom shows **you** the way to uncover and discover your talents by opening your understanding of you wisdom, talents, and innovative ingenuity, allowing you to feel your emotions and energize your brainpower opened the way for me myself and I experience your desired outcomes.

I introduce you to a visionary vocabulary of expand, energize, enterprise and experience life **your** way by understanding the simple fact that everything occurs in the "now," liberating you from your thinking mind.

Robert A. Wilson
Cowboy Wisdom

http://mycowboywisdom.com
Author Page: www.amazon.com/author/robertawilson
Email: Robert@mycowboywisdom.com
https://store.bookbaby.com/book/Dissolving-Pleasing-Others